To Be Alone

The Sweet & Bittersweet

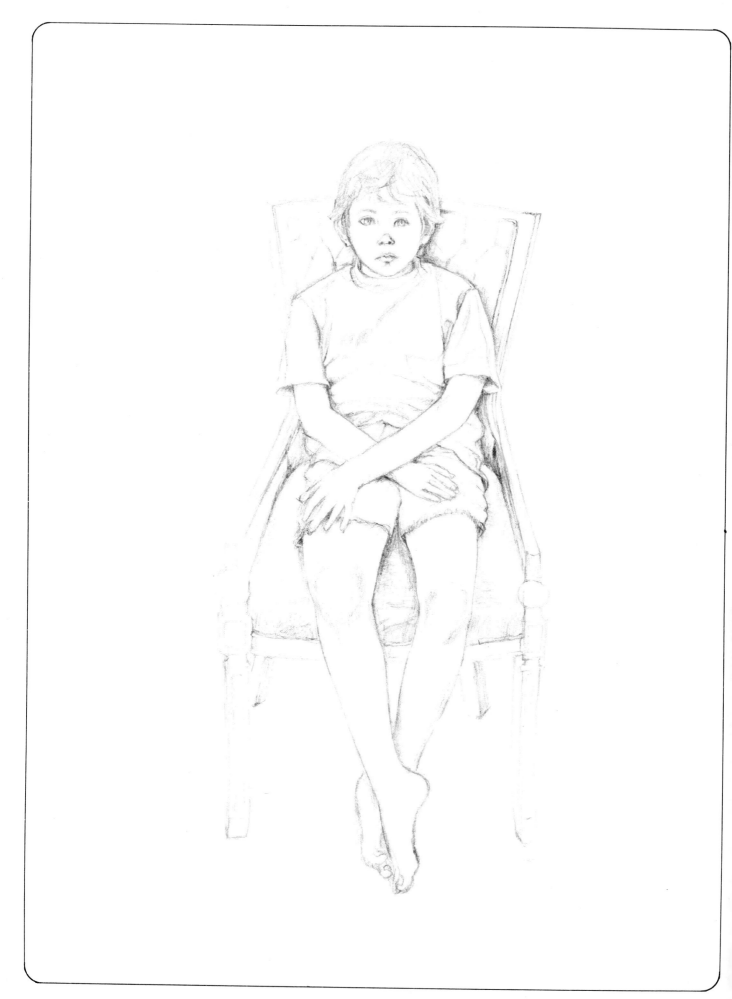

To Be Alone

The Sweet & Bittersweet

An Anthology Selected and Illustrated by

JOAN BERG VICTOR

Crown Publishers, Inc.   New York

Books by Joan Berg Victor

To Be Alone
A Time to Love
Do You Really Love Me?

Children's books:
Bigger Than an Elephant
Where Is My Monster?
The World Is Round

Book design by Carol Callaway

Acknowledgments

The author gratefully acknowledges permission to use the following copyrighted material:

"The Meeting" and "Darkness Music" by Muriel Rukeyser. Reprinted by permission of Monica McCall, International Famous Agency. Copyright © 1944, 1972 by Muriel Rukeyser.

From *Wandering* by Hermann Hesse, translated by James Wright, copyright © 1972 by Farrar, Straus & Giroux, Inc.

"It's Good to Sit with People" and "For Anne" by Leonard Cohen. From *Selected Poems* by Leonard Cohen, published by The Viking Press, 1964. Copyright in all countries of the International Copyright Union. All rights reserved. Reprinted by permission of The Viking Press, Inc.

"Two-Volume Novel" by Dorothy Parker. From *Not So Deep as a Well*, copyright © 1936 by Dorothy Parker, published by The Viking Press, Inc.

From "Do You Really Love Me?" by Joan Berg Victor. Copyright © 1971 by Joan Berg Victor. Reprinted by permission of Grosset & Dunlap, Inc.

"Self" by Norman Henry Pritchard II. From *The Matrix* by Norman Henry Pritchard II, Doubleday and Company, Inc. Copyright © 1963 by Norman Henry Pritchard.

"All of Us Always Turning Away for Solace" by Delmore Schwartz. From *Selected Poems* and *Summer Knowledge*. Copyright © 1938 by New Directions Publishing Corporation. Reprinted by permission of New Directions Publishing Corporation.

"A Letter" by James Dickey. Copyright © 1962 by James Dickey. Reprinted from *Poems 1957-1967* by James Dickey, by permission of Wesleyan University Press.

"After a Train Journey" by May Sarton. Reprinted by permission of Russell & Volkening, Inc., as agents for the author. Copyright © 1948 by May Sarton.

"Waiting" and "Ghost House" by Robert Frost. From *The Poetry of Robert Frost*, edited by Edward Connery Lathem. Copyright © 1934, 1969 by Holt, Rinehart and Winston, Inc. Copyright ® 1962 by Robert Frost. Reprinted by permission of Holt, Rinehart and Winston, Inc.

"Lonesome Boy Blues" by Kenneth Patchen. From *Collected Poems*, copyright © 1952 by Kenneth Patchen. Reprinted by permission of New Directions Publishing Corporation.

From "Petronius Arbiter" #8, translated by Kenneth Rexroth. From Kenneth Rexroth, *The Signature of All Things*, published by New Directions, 1949. All rights reserved. Reprinted by permission of New Directions Publishing Corporation.

From *The Notebooks of Dylan Thomas*. Copyright © 1967 by the Trustees for the Copyright of Dylan Thomas. Reprinted by permission of New Directions Publishing Corporation.

Contents

To Be Alone

The Sweet & Bittersweet

For my children and all my friends who have
touched me and made the world a less lonely place

TO BE ALONE

TO BE ALONE is the glorious anticipation of the time
between meetings; it is the dreadful loneliness of a
rejected lover, a feeling of isolation and alienation.
TO BE ALONE is also a chosen and serene aloneness.

What are you thinking? Please, tell me.
You sitting there, I here and so close.
I am tired of me. I want to get outside of me.
Help me.
Talk to me.
I don't want to be alone.

—Joan Berg Victor

THE MEETING

One o'clock in the letter-box
Very black and I will go home early.
Now I have put off my dancing-dress
And over a sheet of distance write my love.
I walk in the city with my pride of theme
While the lean girls at their betrayal smiling
Dance, do their sea-green dance, and laugh in dancing.
And all the stars fade out of my sky.

Early in the morning on a windy ocean.
My sleep opens upon your face to kiss and find
And take diversion of the meeting waters,
The flameless sky of peace, blue-sided white air.
I leave you as the trivial birds careen
In separation, a dream of easy parting.
I see you through a door.   The door sails away,
And all the ships move into the real sea.

Let that far day arrive, that evening stain!
Down the alleys of the night I trail a cloak;
Field-dusk and mountain-dusk and final darkness—
Each absence brings me nearer to that night
When I stone-still in desire standing
Shall see the masked body of love enter the garden
To reach the night-burning, the perpetual fountain.
And all the birds fly out of my scene.

—*Muriel Rukeyser*

From *WANDERING*

For me, trees have always been the most penetrating preachers. I revere them when they live in tribes and families, in forests and groves. And even more I revere them when they stand alone. They are like lonely persons. Not like hermits who have stolen away out of some weakness, but like great, solitary men, like Beethoven and Nietzsche. In their highest boughs the world rustles, their roots rest in infinity; but they do not lose themselves there, they struggle with all the force of their lives for one thing only: to fulfill themselves according to their own laws, to build up their own form, to represent themselves. Nothing is holier, nothing is more exemplary than a beautiful, strong tree. When a tree is cut down and reveals its naked death-wound to the sun, one can read its whole history in the luminous, inscribed disk of its trunk: in the rings of its years, its scars, all the struggle, all the suffering, all the sickness, all the happiness and prosperity stand truly written, the narrow years and the luxurious years, the attacks withstood, the storms endured. And every young farmboy knows that the hardest and noblest wood has the narrowest rings, that high on the mountains and in continuing danger the most indestructible, the strongest, the ideal trees grow.

Trees are sanctuaries. Whoever knows how to speak to them, whoever knows how to listen to them, can learn the truth. They do not preach learning and precepts, they preach, undeterred by particulars, the ancient law of life.

A tree says: A kernel is hidden in me, a spark, a thought, I am life from eternal life. The attempt and the risk that the eternal mother took with me is unique, unique the form and veins of my skin, unique the smallest play of leaves in my branches and the smallest scar on my bark. I was made to form and reveal the eternal in my smallest special detail.

A tree says: My strength is trust. I know nothing about my fathers, I know nothing about the thousand children that every year spring out of me. I live out the secret of my seed to the very end, and I care for nothing else. I trust that God is in me. I trust that my labor is holy. Out of this trust I live.

When we are stricken and cannot bear our lives any longer, then a tree has something to say to us: Be still! Be still! Look at me! Life is not easy, life is not difficult. Those are childish thoughts. Let God speak within you, and your thoughts will grow silent. You are anxious because your path leads away from mother and home. But every step and every day lead you back again to the mother. Home is neither here nor there. Home is within you, or home is nowhere at all. . . .

Everything is within you, gold and mud, happiness and pain, the laughter of childhood and the apprehension of death. Say yes to everything, shirk nothing, don't try to lie to yourself. You are not a solid citizen, you are not a Greek, you are not harmonious, or the master of yourself, you are a bird in the storm. Let it storm! Let it drive you! How much you have lied! A thousand times, even in your poems and books, you have played the harmonious man, the wise man, the happy, the enlightened man. In the same way, men attacking in war have played heroes, while their bowels twitched. My God, what a poor ape, what a fencer in the mirror, man is—particularly the artist—particularly the poet—particularly myself! . . .

Like the day between morning and evening, my life falls between my urge to travel and my homesickness. Maybe some day I will have come far enough for travel and distances to become part of my soul, so that I will have their images within me, without having to make them literally real any more. Maybe I will also find that secret home within me where there will be no more flirting with gardens and little red houses. To be at home with myself!

How different life would be! There would be a center, and out of that center all forces would reach. . . .

The world has become lovelier. I am alone, and I don't suffer from my loneliness. I don't want life to be anything other than what it is. I am ready to let myself be baked in the sun till I am done. I am eager to ripen. I am ready to die, ready to be born again.

The world has become lovelier.

—Hermann Hesse

From *THE NOTEBOOKS OF DYLAN THOMAS*

O lonely among many, the gods' man,
Knowing exceeding grief and the gods' sorrow
That, like a razor, skims, cuts, and turns,
Aches till the metal meets the marrow,
You, too, know the exceeding joy
And the triumphant crow of laughter.
Out of a bird's wing writing on a cloud
You capture more than man or woman guesses;
Rarer delight shoots in the blood
At the deft movements of the irises
Growing in public places than man knows;
[There in the sunset and sunrise
Joy lifts its head, wonderful with surprise.
A rarer wonder is than man supposes.]

See, on gravel paths under the harpstrung trees,
Feeling the summer wind, hearing the swans,
Leaning from windows over a length of lawns,
On level hills admiring the sea
[Or the steeples of old towns
Stabbing the changing sky,] he is alone,
Alone complains to the stars.
Who are his friends? The wind is his friend,
The glowworm lights his darkness, and
The snail tells of coming rain.

Poem completed March 31 '33.

WAITING
Afield at Dusk

What things for dream there are when specter-like,
Moving along tall haycocks lightly piled,
I enter alone upon the stubble field,
From which the laborers' voices late have died,
And in the antiphony of afterglow
And rising full moon, sit me down
Upon the full moon's side of the first haycock
And lose myself amid so many alike.

I dream upon the opposing lights of the hour,
Preventing shadow until the moon prevail;
I dream upon the nighthawks peopling heaven,
Each circling each with vague unearthly cry,
Or plunging headlong with fierce twang afar;
And on the bat's mute antics, who would seem
Dimly to have made out my secret place,
Only to lose it when he pirouettes,
And seek it endlessly with purblind haste;
On the last swallow's sweep; and on the rasp
In the abyss of odor and rustle at my back,
That, silenced by my advent, finds once more,
After an interval, his instrument,
And tries once—twice—and thrice if I be there;
And on the worn book of old-golden song
I brought not here to read, it seems, but hold
And freshen in this air of withering sweetness;
But on the memory of one absent most,
For whom these lines when they shall greet her eye.

—Robert Frost

TWO-VOLUME NOVEL

The sun's gone dim, and
    The moon's turned black;
For I loved him, and
    He didn't love back.

—Dorothy Parker

From *A LETTER TO ALINE BERNSTEIN*

"We are strangers and exiles here. I feel it now more certainly than ever—and the only home a man ever has on earth, the only moment when he escapes from the prisms of loneliness, is when he enters into the heart of another person. In all the enormous darkness of living and dying, I see these brave little lights go up—the only hope and reason for it all. . . . I believe in love, and in its power to redeem and save our lives. I believe in the loved one the redeemer and saviour."

—Thomas Wolfe

TWENTY-ONE

Only a day away
the loneliness is unbearable.
How will it be if you are a year gone?

What will happen
if I am not to know again
                    your warm arms
your shoulder next to my face at night
the quiet talk over strong coffee
the chase along the toll beach
                              and oh God
so many things.

I am afraid of being alone now
it happens every time you close the door
or go into the next room
                away from me.

I am like a child again
I can't be left alone.

Hurry.

—Rod McKuen

LONESOME BOY BLUES

Oh nobody's a long time
Nowhere's a big pocket
To put little
Pieces of nice things that

Have never really happened

To anyone except
Those people who were lucky enough
Not to get born
Oh lonesome's a bad place

To get crowded into

With only
Yourself riding back and forth
On
A blind white horse
Along an empty road meeting
All your
Pals face to face

Nobody's a long time

—Kenneth Patchen

THE PREACHER: RUMINATES BEHIND THE SERMON

I think it must be lonely to be God.
Nobody loves a master. No. Despite
The bright hosannas, bright dear-Lords, and bright
Determined reverence of Sundays eyes.

Picture Jehovah striding through the hall
Of His importance, creatures running out
From servant-corners to acclaim, to shout
Appreciation of His merit's glare.

But who walks with Him?—dares to take His arm,
To slap Him on the shoulder, tweak His ear,
Buy Him a Coca-Cola or a beer,
Pooh-pooh His politics, call Him a fool?

Perhaps—who knows?—He tires of looking down.
Those eyes are never lifted. Never straight.
Perhaps sometimes He tires of being great
In solitude. Without a hand to hold.

—Gwendolyn Brooks

From *PETRONIUS ARBITER*

I had just gone to bed
And begun to enjoy the first
Stillness of the night,
And sleep was slowly
Overcoming my eyes,
When savage Love
Jerked me up by the hair,
And threw me about,
And commanded me to stay up all night.
He said, 'You are my slave,
The lover of a thousand girls.
Have you become so tough that you can lie here,
All alone and lonely?'
I jumped up barefoot and half dressed,
And ran off in all directions,
And got nowhere by any of them.
First I ran, and then I lingered,
And at last I was ashamed
To be wandering in the empty streets.
The voices of men,
The roar of traffic,
The songs of birds,
Even the barking of dogs,
Everything was still.
And me alone,
Afraid of my bed and sleep,
Ruled by a mighty lust.

—*Kenneth Rexroth*

From *THE ART OF LOVING*

Man is gifted with reason; he is *life being aware of itself*; he has awareness of himself, of his fellow man, of his past, and of the possibilities of his future. This awareness of himself as a separate entity, the awareness of his own short life span, of the fact that without his will he is born and against his will he dies, that he will die before those whom he loves, or they before him, the awareness of his aloneness and separateness, of his helplessness before the forces of nature and of society, all this makes his separate, disunited existence an unbearable prison. He would become insane could he not liberate himself from this prison and reach out, unite himself in some form or other with men, with the world outside.

—Erich Fromm

THE BEGINNING

So summer comes in the end to these few stains
And the rust and rot of the door through which she went.

The house is empty. But here is where she sat
To comb her dewy hair, a touchless light,

Perplexed by its darker iridescences.
This was the glass in which she used to look

At the moment's being, without history,
The self of summer perfectly perceived,

And feel its country gaiety and smile
And be surprised and tremble, hand and lip.

This is the chair from which she gathered up
Her dress, the carefulest, commodious weave

Inwoven by a weaver to twelve bells . . .
The dress is lying, cast-off, on the floor.

Now, the first tutoyers of tragedy
Speak softly, to begin with, in the eaves.

—*Wallace Stevens*

19

HOME TOWN

I go out like a ghost,
nights, to walk the streets
I walked fifteen years younger—
seeking my old defeats,
devoured by the old hunger,
I had supposed

this longing and upheaval
had left me with my youth.
Fifteen years gone; once more,
the old lies are the truth:
I must prove I dare,
and the world, and love, is evil

I have had loves, had such
honors as freely came;
it does not seem to matter.
Boys swagger just the same
along the curbs, or mutter
among themselves and watch.

They're out for the same prize.
And, as the evening grows,
the young girls take the street,
hard, in harlequin clothes,
with black shells on their feet
and challenge in their eyes.

Like a young bitch in her season
she walked the carnival
tonight, trailed by boys;
then, stopped at a penny stall
for me; by glittering toys
the pitchman called the reason

to come and take a chance,
try my hand, my skill.
I could not look; bereft
of breath, against my will,
I walked ahead and left
her there without one glance.

Pale soul, consumed by fear
of the living world you haunt,
have you learned what habits lead you
to hunt what you don't want;
learned who does not need you;
learned you are no one here?

—*W. D. Snodgrass*

ABSENCE

I visited the place where we last met.
Nothing was changed, the gardens were well-tended,
The fountains sprayed their usual steady jet;
There was no sign that anything had ended
And nothing to instruct me to forget.

The thoughtless birds that shook out of the trees,
Singing an ecstasy I could not share,
Played cunning in my thoughts. Sure in these
Pleasures there could not be a pain to bear
Or any discord shake the level breeze.

It was because the place was just the same
That made your absence seem a savage force,
For under all the gentleness there came
An earthquake tremor: fountain, birds and grass
Were shaken by my thinking of your name.

—Elizabeth Jennings

MOVING IN

I moved into my house one day
In a downpour of leaves and rain,
"I took possession," as they say,
With solitude for my domain.

At first it was an empty place
Where every room I came to meet
Watched me in silence like a face:
I heard the whisper of my feet.

So huge the absence walking there
Beside me on the yellow floor,
That one fly buzzing on the air
But made the stillness more and more.

What I possessed was all my own,
Yet not to be possessed at all,
And not a house or even hearthstone,
And never any sheltering wall.

There solitude became my task,
No shelter but a grave demand,
And I must answer, never ask,
Taking this bridegroom by the hand.

I moved into my life one day
In a downpour of leaves in flood,
I took possession as they say,
And knew I was alone for good.

—May Sarton

24

NOSTALGIA

In cock-wattle sunset or grey
Dawn when the dagger
Points again of longing
For what was never home
We needs must turn away
From the voices that cry 'come'—
That under-sea ding-donging.

Dingle-dongle, bells and bluebells,
Snapdragon solstice, lunar lull,
The wasp circling the honey
Or the lamp soft on the snow—
These are the times at which
The will is vulnerable,
The trigger-finger slow,
The spirit lonely.

These are the times at which
Aloneness is too ripe
When homesick for the hollow
Heart of the Milky Way
The soundless clapper calls
And we would follow
But earth and will are stronger
And nearer—and we stay.

—*Louis MacNeice*

Yet I cannot tarry longer.

The sea that calls all things unto her calls me, and I must embark.

For to stay, though the hours burn in the night, is to freeze and crystallize and be bound in a mould.

Fain would I take with me all that is here. But how shall I?

A voice cannot carry the tongue and the lips that gave it wings. Alone must it seek the ether.

And alone and without his nest shall the eagle fly across the sun.

—Kahlil Gibran

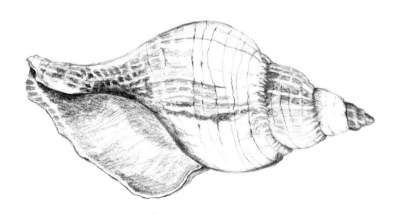

From *THE HILLS BEYOND*

Loneliness, far from being a rare and curious phenomenon . . . is the central and inevitable fact of human existence. When we examine the moments, acts and statements of all kind of people—not only the grief and ecstasy of the greatest poets, but also the huge unhappiness of the average soul, as evidenced by the innumerable strident words of abuse, hatred, contempt, mistrust and scorn that forever grate upon our ears as the manswarm passes us in the streets—we find, I think, that they are all suffering from the same thing. The final cause of their complaint is loneliness.

—Thomas Wolfe

A STONE, A LEAF, A DOOR

. . . A stone, a leaf, an unfound door;
Of a stone, a leaf, a door.
And of all the forgotten faces.

Naked and alone we came into exile.
In her dark womb
We did not know our mother's face;
From the prison of her flesh have we come
Into the unspeakable and incommunicable prison
Of this earth.

Which of us has known his brother?
Which of us has looked into his father's heart?
Which of us has not remained forever prison-pent?
Which of us is not forever a stranger and alone?

O waste of loss, in the hot mazes, lost,
Among bright stars
On this most weary unbright cinder, lost!
Remembering speechlessly
We seek the great forgotten language,
The lost lane-end into heaven,
A stone, a leaf, an unfound door.

—Thomas Wolfe

From *THE CONQUEST OF LONELINESS*

Loneliness is not the disease of being alone; being alone is in the deepest sense the human condition. It is the disease of feeling alone, of feeling isolated, cut off from human contact and human warmth. Some people battle all their lives against this poignant emotion, struggling constantly to come to terms with the immutable fact of their existence: the fact that all human beings are separate, one from another, and will remain so all their lives; each sealed within the thin envelope of skin in which he is contained. If this struggle is successful, the individual ultimately transcends that physical limitation and becomes most himself precisely because he is closely bound to others.

—Eric P. Mosse, M.D.

A CERTAIN PEACE

it was very pleasant
not having you around
this afternoon

not that i don't love you
and want you and need you
and love loving and wanting
        and needing you
but there was a certain peace
when you walked out the door
and i knew you would do
        something
you wanted to do
and i could run
a tub full of water
and not worry about answering
        the phone
for your call
and soak in bubbles
and not worry whether you would
        want something
special for dinner
and rub lotion all over me
for as long as i wanted
and not worry if you had
        a good idea
or wanted to use the bathroom

and there was a certain
        excitement
when after midnight
you came home
and we had coffee
and i had a day of mine
that made me as happy
as yours did you

        —Nikki Giovanni

32

From *DO YOU REALLY LOVE ME?*

Before you, things were quite the same.
Before—
I was very afraid of tomorrow.
I was very afraid of being alone.
I hated not caring.
I hated feeling empty
No, maybe things were not the same.

Before—my stomach didn't get a hollow feeling
every time the phone rang—
I didn't look at the clock a hundred times a
day waiting for tomorrow—the day I could see you—
to come.
Before you—I could eat and sleep—
and feel empty—
and lonely
and dead inside.

The fragrance from your yellow rose fills the dining
room as I sit here and work.
You—all of you—fills me until I think I cannot
bear it.
I put my hand to my face and I smell of you.
You are everywhere.

I wanted to be one with you
with someone—
And the more I wanted to lose myself
the more I was aware of me—
Me isolated.

I am part of the whole cycle—
I'm not alone.

—Joan Berg Victor

NO LETTER

Be angry yourself, as well you may,
But why with her? She is no party to
Those avaricious dreams that pester you.
Why knot your fists as though plotting to slay
Even our postman George (whose only due
Is a small Christmas box on Christmas Day)
If his delivery does not raise the curse
Of doubt from your impoverished universe?

—Robert Graves

FOR THE LONELY
(At Christmas)

The lonely ones will pass this way,
Arrange a window's bright display
Of crimson candles shining clear—
This is their bitter day.

To them the sound of noisy cheer
Falls desolately on the ear
A focussed loneliness now lies
Against the empty year.

This is the hour of homely ties
Renewed in love, with meeting eyes:
Today no differences mar
The peace we symbolize.

Fasten the balsam's topmost star
To shed its tiny glow afar
Calling the lonely ones who pass—
And leave the door ajar.

—Helen Frith Stickney

XXI

Streets and the solitude of country places
Were once his friends. But as a man born blind,
Opening his eyes from lovely dreams, might find
The world a desert and men's larval faces
So hateful, he would wish to seek again
The darkness and his old chimeric sight
Of beauties inward—so, that fresh delight,
Vision of bright fields and angelic men,
That love which made him all the world, is gone.
Hating and hated now, he stands alone,
An island-point, measureless gulfs apart
From other lives, from the old happiness
Of being more than self, when heart to heart
Gave all, yet grew the greater, not the less.

—*Aldous Huxley*

From *MAN'S SEARCH FOR HIMSELF*

Loneliness is such an omnipotent and painful threat to many persons that they have little conception of the positive values of solitude, and even at times are very frightened at the prospect of being alone. Many people suffer from "the fear of finding oneself alone," remarks André Gide, "and so they don't find themselves at all."

—*Rollo May*

AFTER A TRAIN JOURNEY

My eyes are full of rivers and trees tonight,
The clear waters sprung in the green,
The swan's neck flashing in sunlight,
The trees laced dark, the tiny unknown flowers,
Skies never still, shining and darkening the hours.
How can I tell you all that I have been?

My thoughts are rooted with the trees,
My thoughts flow with the stream.
They flow and are arrested as a frieze.
How can I answer now or tell my dream,
How tell you what is far and what is near?
Only that river, tree and swan are here.

Even at the slow rising of the full moon,
That delicate disturber of the soul,
I am so drenched in rivers and in trees,
I cannot speak. I have nothing to tell,
Except that I must learn of this pure solitude
All that I am and might be, root and bone,
Flowing and still and beautiful and good,
Now I am almost earth and almost whole.

—May Sarton

IT'S GOOD TO SIT WITH PEOPLE

It's good to sit with people
        who are up so late
your other homes wash away
and other meals you left
        unfinished on the plate
It's just coffee
        and a piano player's cigarette
and Tim Hardin's song
and the song in your head
        that always makes you wait
I'm thinking of you
        little Frédérique
with your white white skin
and your stories of wealth
        in Normandy
I don't think I ever told you
that I wanted to save the world
watching television
        while we made love
ordering Greek wine and olives for you
while my friend scattered
dollar bills over the head
of the belly-dancer
under the clarinettes of Eighth Avenue
listening to your plans
for an exclusive pet shop in Paris
        Your mother telephoned me
she said I was too old for you
and I agreed
but you came to my room
one morning after a long time
because you said you loved me
        From time to time I meet men
who said they gave you money
and some girls have said
that you weren't really a model
Don't they know what it means
to be lonely
lonely for boiled eggs in silver cups
lonely for a large dog
who obeys your voice
lonely for rain in Normandy
seen through leaded windows

lonely for a fast car
lonely for restaurant asparagus
lonely for a simple prince
and an explorer
I'm sure they know
but we are all creatures of envy
we need our stone fingernails
on another's beauty
we demand the hidden love
of everyone we meet
the hidden love not the daily love
        Your breasts are beautiful
warm porcelain taste
of worship and greed
        Your eyes come to me
under the perfect spikes
of imperishable eyelashes
        Your mouth living
on French words
and the soft ashes of your make-up
Only with you
        I did not imitate myself
only with you
        I asked for nothing
your long long fingers
deciphering your hair
        your lace blouse
borrowed from a photographer
the bathroom lights
flashing on your new red fingernails
your tall legs at attention
        as I watch you from my bed
while you brush dew
        from the mirror
to work behind the enemy lines
        of your masterpiece
Come to me if you grow old
come to me if you need coffee

—*Leonard Cohen*

FOR ANNE

With Annie gone,
Whose eyes to compare
With the morning sun?

Not that I did compare,
But I do compare
Now that she's gone.

—Leonard Cohen

SONNET

Two years have passed, and made a perfect wheel
Of all that love can know of joy and pain.
All that lovers hope or dread to feel
We've felt, and are arrived at naught again.
On barren earth the sky has loosed its rain
Too generously: last year's abundant yield
Now straggles up, a green and scattered stain
Across the drenched exhaustion of the field.

So, let us leave off trying, now, to mend
A chain long broken; let us play no more
At being firmly bound: love's at an end
And cannot live again. Oh, set no stars
On other loves; all love's ceaseless bend
From naught to naught; farewell: make fast your door.

—*James Agee*

A LETTER.

Looking out of the dark of the town
At midnight, looking down
Into water under the lighthouse:
Abstractedly, timelessly looking
For something beneath the jetty,
Waiting for the dazed, silent flash,

Like the painless explosion that kills one,
To come from above and slide over
And empty the surface for miles—
The useless, imperial sweep
Of utter light—you see
A thicket of little fish

Below the squared stone of your window,
Catching, as it passes,
The blue afterthought of the blaze.
Shone almost into full being,
Inlaid in frail gold in their floor,
Their collected vision sways

Like dust among them
You can see the essential spark
Of sight, of intuition,
Travel from eye to eye.
The next leg of light that comes round
Shows nothing where they have been,

But words light up in the head
To take their deep place in the darkness,
Arcing quickly from image to image
Like mica catching the sun:
The words of a love letter,
Of a letter to a long-dead father,

To an unborn son, to a woman
Long another man's wife, to her children,
To anyone out of reach, not born,
Or dead, who lives again,
Is born, is young, is the same:
Anyone who can wait no longer

Beneath the huge blackness of time
Which lies concealing, concealing
What must gleam forth in the end,
Glimpsed, unchanging, and gone
When memory stands without sleep
And gets its strange spark from the world.

—*James Dickey*

DARKNESS MUSIC

The days grow and the stars cross over
Drawing you nightly
Along my human love.
Alone at the vertical wall and wild with tears
I watch your line of windows.
Dance of eyes,
Their constellation steers me from my death,
Away, persuading me of
Wavering dawn.
Breeze of lilac in the sleepless night;
Here overflown by bells
Black altitudes,
And my wild bed turns slowly among the stars.

—*Muriel Rukeyser*

TWENTY

People riding trains are nice
they offer magazines
and chocolate-covered cherries,
the details you want most to know
      about their recent operations.
If I'd been riding home to you
I could have listened with both ears
but I was on my way away.

Across from me
there was a girl crying
      (long, silent tears)
while an old man held her hand.
It was only a while ago you said,
Take the seat by the window,
      you'll see more.

I filled the seat beside me
with my coat and books.
I'm antisocial without you.
I'm antiworld and people too.

Sometimes I think
I'll never ride a train again.
At least not away.

      —Rod McKuen

SUNDAY EVENING

We are two acquaintances on a train,
Rattling back through darkening twilight suburbs
From a weekend in the country, into town.
The station lights flare past us, and we glance
Furtively at our watches, sit upright
On leather benches in the smoke-dim car
And try to make appropriate conversation.

We come from similar streets in the same city
And have spent this same hiatus of three days
Escaping streets and lives that we have chosen.
Escape by deck chairs sprawled on evening lawns,
By citronella and by visitant moths;
Escape by sand and water in the eyes,
And sea-noise drowned in weekend conversation.

Uneasy, almost, that we meet again,
Impatient for this rattling ride to end,
We still are stricken with a dread of passing
Time, the coming loneliness of travelers
Parting in hollow stations, going home
To silent rooms in too-familiar streets
With unknown footsteps pacing overhead.

For there are things we might have talked about,
And there are signs we might have shared in common.
We look out vainly at the passing stations
As if some lamplit shed or gleaming roof
Might reawake the sign in both of us.
But this is only Rye or Darien,
And whoever we both knew there has moved away.

And I suppose there never will be time
To speak of more than this—the change in weather,
The lateness of the train on Sunday evenings—
Never enough or always too much time.
Life lurches past us like a windowed twilight
Seen from a train that halts at little junctions
Where weekend half-acquaintances say good-by.

—Adrienne Rich

Part II of THE AURORAS OF AUTUMN

Farewell to an idea . . . A cabin stands,
Deserted, on a beach. It is white,
As by a custom or according to

An ancestral theme or as a consequence
Of an infinite course. The flowers against the wall
Are white, a little dried, a kind of mark

Reminding, trying to remind, of a white
That was different, something else, last year
Or before, not the white of an aging afternoon,

Whether fresher or duller, whether of winter cloud
Or of winter sky, from horizon to horizon.
The wind is blowing the sand across the floor.

Here, being visible is being white,
Is being of the solid of white, the accomplishment
Of an extremist in an exercise . . .

The season changes. A cold wind chills the beach.
The long lines of it grow longer, emptier,
A darkness gathers though it does not fall

And the whiteness grows less vivid on the wall.
The man who is walking turns blankly on the sand.
He observes how the north is always enlarging the change.

With its frigid brilliances, its blue-red sweeps
And gusts of great enkindlings, its polar green,
The color of ice and fire and solitude.

—*Wallace Stevens*

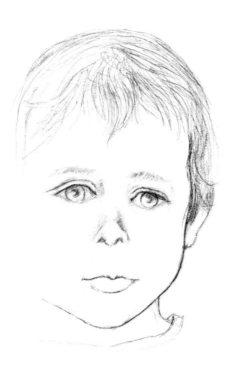

THE TWO-YEAR-OLD HAS HAD A MOTHERLESS WEEK

The two-year-old has had a motherless week. Mother has gone to bring
back the baby. A week is many many years. One evening they
bring the news to the playpen: a child is born, you have a baby
brother. The dark little eyes consider this news and convey no
message. One day long after, they arrive in a taxi, father, mother,
bundle. The two-year-old observes from her blue walker on the
sunny sidewalk. She stares and turns away on her wheels.

The father has gone to the other side of the world. He will bring back
strange presents to a strange house. The little ones shyly wait their
turn. Reconciliation is gradual.

In Trenton, New Jersey, the soldiers sit in the innocuous bar. It's three
years since they saw the ones they wrote to. They are all afraid to
go home. One lives two blocks away; he is very silent. Late in the
afternoon, at an ungiven signal, they get up and disperse, like
criminals perfectly trained for the job ahead.

In my brother's house when I left (whole histories ago) the furniture
was honeymoon fresh, gleam of ceramics; soft beige carpets smelt
like new-mown hay. With a shock I see the carpet is worn; the sofa
has settled; books have changed places. A thousand days of words
have passed.

Time is mostly absences, oceans generally at peace, and lives we love
most often out of reach.

—Karl Shapiro

NIGHT SCENE

I leave your house, turn back
Away from night's blind black
Toward that pale window where
I see your loved face stare:
Dear dazzle whose live white
In that ecstatic night
Shames the electric light.

You do not know I see
Your eyes that look for me.
You find night empty, stand
And wave your empty hand:
Then like a child, but slow
As if in fear, you blow
A kiss to the dark and go.

I do not know why such
Brief act without warm touch
Should stop a man stone still
And shake him like a chill
On one warm summer night:
A woman's gesture, slight
And quick as sudden light.

So in that empty air
I fill with rage that there
I left the wonder of
Your silhouetted love:
Bewilderment of eye
More passionate than cry
That moves one thigh to thigh.

—Paul Engle

ALL OF US ALWAYS TURNING AWAY FOR SOLACE

All of us always turning away for solace

From the lonely room where the self must be honest,
All of us turning from being alone (at best
Boring) because what we want most is to be
Interested,
    play billiards, poking a ball
On the table, play baseball, batting a ball
On the diamond, play football, kicking a ball
On the gridiron,
     seventy thousand applauding.

This amuses, this indeed is our solace:
Follow the bouncing ball! O, fellow, follow,
See what is here and clear, one thing repeated,
Bounding, evasive, caught and uncaught, fumbled
—Follow the bouncing ball and thus you follow,
Fingering closely your breast on the left side,

The bouncing ball you turned from for solace.

—Delmore Schwartz

GHOST HOUSE

I dwell in a lonely house I know
That vanished many a summer ago,
And left no trace but the cellar walls,
And a cellar in which the daylight falls,
And the purple-stemmed wild raspberries grow.

O'er ruined fences the grapevines shield
The woods come back to the mowing field;
The orchard tree has grown one copse
Of new wood and old where the woodpecker chops;
The footpath down to the well is healed.

I dwell with a strangely aching heart
In that vanished abode there far apart
On that disused and forgotten road
That has no dust-bath now for the toad.
Night comes; the black bats tumble and dart;

The whippoorwill is coming to shout
And hush and cluck and flutter about:
I hear him begin far enough away
Full many a time to say his say
Before he arrives to say it out.

It is under the small, dim, summer star.
I know not who these mute folk are
Who share the unlit place with me—
Those stones out under the low-limbed tree
Doubtless bear names that the mosses mar.

They are tireless folk, but slow and sad,
Though two, close-keeping, are lass and lad,—
With none among them that ever sings,
And yet, in view of how many things,
As sweet companions as might be had.

—Robert Frost

58

From *STOLEN APPLES*

Damp white imprints dog the feet;
snowbound trolley, snowbound street.
Her tip of glove to lip and cheek,
"Goodby." Go.
Deathly, into soaring snow
and stillness, as expected go.
A turn:
        the plunge to the metro,
A blare of lights. A melting hat.
I stand, am spun in drafts, see black
take the tunnel, train, and track,
sit and wait as others sat,
touch cold marble, chill my hand
and, heavy-hearted, understand
that nothing ever really happened,
ever would, ever can.

—Yevgeni Yevtushenko
Translated by Anthony Kahn

From *A PSYCHOLOGIST LOOKS AT LOVE*

"Love is, I think, the most successful attempt to escape our loneliness and isolation. It is an illusion like every search for human perfection, but it is the most necessary illusion of our culture. . . . To connect one's life in thoughts and deeds with others is the only way to make it worth living."

—Theodor Reik

WINDOW

They share this window:
Rain smokes down between trees
And soil drinks.

Hands burn bushes that cannot be reached
Scorch rain
Turn to smoke that drifts around leaves.
The sky eases his skull.

Air moves, disguised as rain, between
Trees that caught her glance
That passed between them in this wooden house
These bones of wax
That widening ink-split of the sky
Fast running out—

They call it love
A vicious loneliness
An only child of forest and retreat
Which makes her laugh (and him)
Love, and his consort, love
When her glowing eyes turn.

—Alan Sillitoe

From *FELIXSTOWE, OR THE LAST OF HER ORDER*

Across the grass the poplar shades grow longer
And louder clang the waves along the coast.
The band packs up. The evening breeze is stronger
And all the world goes home to tea and toast.
I hurry past a cakeshop's tempting scones
Bound for the red brick twilight of St. John's.

"Thou knowest my down sitting and mine uprising"
Here where the white light burns with steady glow
Safe from the vain world's silly sympathizing,
Safe with the Love that I was born to know,
Safe from the surging of the lonely sea
My heart finds rest, my heart finds rest in Thee.

—*John Betjeman*

From *PRELUDE FOR MEMNON*

Then came I to the shoreless shore of silence,
Where never summer was nor shade of tree,
Nor sound of water, nor sweet light of sun,
But only nothing and the shore of nothing,
Above, below, around, and in my heart:

Where day was not, not night, nor space, nor time,
Where no bird sang, save him of memory,
Nor footstep marked upon the marl, to guide
My halting footstep; and I turned for terror,
Seeking in vain the Pole Star of my thought;

Where it was blown among the shapeless clouds,
And gone as soon as seen, and scarce recalled,
Its image lost and I directionless;
Alone upon the brown sad edge of chaos,
In the wan evening that was evening always;

Then closed my eyes upon the sea of nothing
While memory brought back a sea more bright,
With long, long waves of light, and the swift sun,
And the good trees that bowed upon the wind;
And stood until grown dizzy with that dream;

Seeking in all that joy of things remembered
One image, one the dearest, one most bright,
One face, one star, one daisy, one delight,
One hour with wings most heavenly and swift,
One hand the tenderest upon my heart;

But still no image came, save of that sea,
No tenderer thing than thought of tenderness,
No heart or daisy brighter than the rest;
And only sadness at the bright sea lost,
And mournfulness that all had not been praised.

O lords of chaos, atoms of desire,
Whirlwind of fruitfulness, destruction's seed,
Hear now upon the void my late delight,
The quick brief cry of memory, that knows
At the dark's edge how great the darkness is.

—*Conrad Aiken*

INCANTATION

Think of me on spring nights
and think of me on summer nights,
think of me on autumn nights
and think of me on winter nights.
Though I'm not there, but somewhere gone,
far from your side, as if abroad,
stretch yourself on the long cool sheet,
float on your back, as in the sea,
surrendering to the soft slow wave,
with me, as with the sea, utterly alone.

I want nothing on your mind all day.
Let the day turn everything upside down,
besmudge with smoke and flood with wine,
distract you till I fade from view.
All right, think of anything by day,
but in the night—only of me alone.

Over the locomotive whistles, over
the wind, ripping the clouds to shreds,
listen to me, for pity's sake:
show me again, in the narrow room,
your eyes half-shut with ecstasy and pain,
your palms pressing your temples till they ache.

I beseech you—in the stillest stillness,
or when the rain patters on your roof,
or the snow sparks on your windowpanes,
and you lie between sleep and waking—
think of me on spring nights
and think of me on summer nights,
think of me on autumn nights
and think of me on winter nights.

—*Yevgeni Yevtushenko*
Translated by Stanley Kunitz with Anthony Kahn

WE PICK SOME UNSUSPECTING SOUL

We pick some unsuspecting soul, usually a friend, on whom to visit a lifetime of frustration. Usually a friend, at one fell swoop. That's what friends are for.

Incapable of loyalty, I marvel at it, imitate it nicely. But the feeling comes from outside. It doesn't sprout in my own soil. I carry it from a florist of sorts, some man or woman of character, and tend it lovingly. It struggles manfully in my slant sun, flourishes in the room where I am. I scat the cat away with a loud newspaper. All my plants are exotics, bamboo, rubber, cocoa, some with names I have never found out. They do well in the hothouse of my eye; they bring admiring glances. I sketch the shadows now and then.

At the bottom of the rubber plant one great leaf is dying an interesting death. It dies with astonishing rapidity. Monday, a few dabs of bright yellow. Tuesday, a ladder of yellow on one side. Wednesday, half green, half yellow, split down the middle. Thursday a spot of deadly brown. Then the whole thing twists to a Dead Sea Scroll of deadness. A single new leaf will take a month to come.

What you say is true: I have no friends.

—*Karl Shapiro*

UNWANTED

The poster with my picture on it
Is hanging on the bulletin board in the Post Office.

I stand by it hoping to be recognized
Posing first full face and then profile

But everybody passes by and I have to admit
The photograph was taken some years ago.

I was unwanted then I'm unwanted now
Ah guess ah'll go up echo mountain and crah.

I wish someone would find my fingerprints somewhere
Maybe on a corpse and say, You're it.

Description: Male, or reasonably so
White, but not lily-white and usually deep-red

Thirty-fivish, and looks it lately
Five-feet-nine and one-hundred-thirty pounds: no physique

Black hair going gray, hairline receding fast
What used to be curly, now fuzzy

Brown eyes starey under beetling brow
Mole on chin, probably will become a wen

It is perfectly obvious that he was not popular at school
No good at baseball, and wet his bed.

His aliases tell his history: Dumbell, Good-for-nothing,
Jewboy, Fieldinsky, Skinny, Fierce Face, Greaseball, Sissy.

Warning: This man is not dangerous, answers to any name
Responds to love, don't call him or he will come.

—Edward Field

PERSHORE STATION,
OR A LIVERISH JOURNEY FIRST CLASS

The train at Pershore station was waiting that Sunday night

Gas light on the platform, in my carriage electric light,

Gas light on frosty evergreens, electric on Empire wood,

The Victorian world and the present in a moment's neigh-
bourhood

There was no one about but a conscript who was saying
good-bye to his love

On the windy weedy platform with the sprinkled stars above

When sudden the waiting stillness shook with the ancient
spells

Of an older world than all our worlds in the sound of the
Pershore bells.

They were ringing them down for Evensong in the lighted
abbey near,

Sounds which had poured through apple boughs for seven
centuries here.

With Guilt, Remorse, Eternity the void within me fills

And I thought of her left behind me in the Herefordshire
Hills.

I remembered her defencelessness as I made my heart a
stone.

Till she wove her self-protection round and left me on my
own.

And plunged in a deep self pity I dreamed of another wife

And lusted for freckled faces and lived a separate life.

One word would have made her love me, one word would
have made her turn

But the word I never murmured and now I am left to burn.

Evesham, Oxford and London. The carriage is new and
smart.

I am cushioned and soft and heated with a deadweight in
my heart.

—*John Betjeman*

NOBODY RIDING THE ROADS TODAY

Nobody riding the roads today
But I hear the living rush
far away from my heart

Nobody meeting on the streets
But I rage from the crowded
overtones of emptiness

Nobody sleeping in my bed
But I breathe like windows
broken by emergencies

Nobody laughing anymore
But I see the world split
and twisted up like open stone

Nobody riding the roads today
But I hear the living rush
far away from my heart

—June Jordan

CREEK SONG

As she walked by Unami
that told her where it went
by the pounding blood of its autumn mud,
her eyes of sixteen
looked, against her eyelids,
at dark blood of her own
that frightened her and lightened her
and made her want to sing.

As she walked by Unami
in the mid-August heat,
she held her hands like hard breastbands
over her restless breath.
The pike that swam the ripples
slowed its pulsing fin,
and its mottled spear rushed at her
and so her hands dropped down.

As she walked by Unami
on the first of May, she saw
darkness pour from a sycamore
as if from a wound.
It might have been a shadow
or wind in opening buds,
but she had to close her staring eyes
to stop the rising mist.

As she walked by Unami
on a crust of fallen snow,
she touched the splice of forming ice
over the current's flow.
Her arms within her coat sleeves,
her blood within her arms,
cooled like the creek, had learned to keep
beyond the reach of storms.

—*Millen Brand*

THE HUT

And once again a fisherman's hut
opening to me late in the night,
suddenly as much a part of me
as the one along whose floor I used to crawl.

Quietly I lay down in the corner
as if it were my old lost place:—
that shaky, chinky floor,
whose every crack and knot I knew.

And I was home again, painfully at home,
amid the smells of fish and tobacco,
children, kittens, borscht,
fumes rising, purifying.

Already the room rocked with the fisherman's snores;
the children already had climbed into their bunks,
their teeth nibbling
on steamy pancakes.

Nobody but the housewife stirred,
washing, scrubbing.
A poker, a broom, a needle—
there must always be something in her hands.

Outside a storm was brewing on the Pechora:
you could hear the river seethe.
"She's kicking up her heels," she said,
as if speaking of a coffee-colored cow.

A puff, blowing out the smoky lamp,
left the room to its own darkness.
I could hear the slap-slosh sound
of her laundry chores in the kitchen.

An old clock creaked in the night,
dragging the weight of history.
From the freshly laid kindling
a white fire broke and crackled.

And, full of wonder and fear,
untamed, from the shadows,
eight children's eyes gleamed
like eight sprays from your waters, Pechora.

They leaned out over their bunks
from an impossibly distant distance,
four little selves (myself)
watching a grown-up, me.

A silent prayer crossed my lips,
as I lay still, pretending to sleep.
And the kitchen noises stopped:
I heard the door squeak open.

And in this depth of solitude,
through the veil of this slumber,
I felt the touch of something
remembered from my childhood.

A sheepskin coat—that's what it was—
thrown on me snugly, shaggily, warmly
and a moment later, from the kitchen tub,
the slapping of the clothes again.

I could almost see those hands dancing
through diapers, bedsheets, dungarees,
to the music of all our passions,
to the roar of world events.

Certainly more than one pretentious nonentity
had wormed his rotten way into eternity,
but only this recurring slap-slosh
struck me, in essence, as eternal.

And a teeming sense of fate
overwhelmed me,
like the exhalation of a hut
where life lies heavy on millions of women,

and where—who knows when?—
after the mastery has been won,
a million little selves (myself)
will watch a grown-up, me.

—*Yevgeni Yevtushenko*

Translated by Stanley Kunitz
    with Anthony Kahn

THE REMEMBRANCE

I have forgotten you. There is grey light on my
Hands and I have forgotten you. There is light enough.
There is light enough left to forget your face by,
Voice by, to forget you. As long as the
Light lasts on my hands I forget you.
There needs be some light: a little.
A man remembers by night—even the
Windows barely a sure shape and the
Shadows anything, standing for anything.
Night is never alone, it remembers.
At night the hair mouth eyes—
The eyes—at night they return to us.

Between the night and me this light,
Little enough, a thin cover,
Fragile defense against the meaning dark
Where eyes are always but not seen till night comes.
Now for a little there is light between.

—*Archibald MacLeish*

THE REWARDS OF LIVING A SOLITARY LIFE

"Alone one is never lonely: the spirit adventures, waking/In a quiet garden, in a cool house, abiding single there."

Loneliness is most acutely felt with other people . . . Alone we can afford to be wholly whatever we are, and to feel whatever we feel absolutely. That is a great luxury!

I am lonely only when I am overtired, when I have worked too long without a break, when for the time being I feel empty and need filling up. And I am lonely sometimes when I come back home after a lecture trip, when I have seen a lot of people and talked a lot, and am full to the brim with experience that needs to be sorted out.

Then for a little while the house feels huge and empty, and I wonder where my self is hiding. It has to be recaptured slowly by watering the plants, perhaps, and looking again at each one as though it were a person, by feeding the two cats, by cooking a meal.

It takes a while, as I watch the surf blowing up in fountains at the end of the field, but the moment comes when the world falls away, and the self emerges again from the deep unconscious, bringing back all I have recently experienced to be explored and slowly understood, when I can converse again with my own hidden powers, and so grow, and so be renewed, till death do us part.

—May Sarton

STRAW FOR THE FIRE

What dies before me is myself alone:
What lives again? Only a man of straw—
Yet straw can feed a fire to melt down stone.

You can't talk away from your own shadow;
I have observed the quiet around the opening flower,
The numinous ring surrounding the bud-sheaths . . .
The point is, dear father, if I don't stop soon,
I'm going to become a sun-tanned idiot boy . . .
I have basted the meat and eaten the bones;
I've kept grandpa from crying into his beard;
All I ask is a way out of slop;
Loose me into grace, papa . . .

The feeling: you are alone in the room.
If you turn around you will not be there.

Loneliness is a strange, pitiless teacher.

—*Theodore Roethke*

k

DATE DUE
